DATE DUE

FEB 15 2001

Return Material Promptly

COPY 8

J
624.55
P

Pelta, Kathy.
Bridging the Golden Gate / by Kathy Pelta. -- Minneapolis : Lerner Publications Co., c1987.

96 p. : ill. ; bkl 4-6.

88590

Includes index.
SUMMARY: Details the story of the building of the bridge across the entrance to San Francisco Bay, once the longest and tallest bridge, but still beautiful and famous.
ISBN 0-8225-1707-8(lib. bdg.) : $10.95

1. Golden Gate Bridge (San Francisco, Calif.) I. Title.

3 DEC 88

86-21077 /AC

Bridging the Golden Gate

Bridging the Golden Gate

by Kathy Pelta

Lerner Publications Company • Minneapolis

ACKNOWLEDGEMENTS

For their help, thanks to Norma Flanery and Stu Nixon (Redwood Empire Association); Patricia Akre (San Francisco Archives); Irene Stachura (National Maritime Museum Library); Bob David, Linda Ploof, Trubee Schock, and Bruce Selby (Golden Gate Bridge, Highway and Transportation District); and Richard Dillon, Ruth Natusch, and John Strickland.

Copyright © 1987 by Kathy Pelta

All rights reserved. International copyright secured. No part of this book may be reproduced or transmitted in any form or by any means, electronic or mechanical, including photocopying and recording, or by any information storage or retrieval system, without permission in writing from the publisher, except for the inclusion of brief quotations in an acknowledged review.

Manufactured in the United States of America

LIBRARY OF CONGRESS CATALOGING-IN-PUBLICATION DATA

Pelta, Kathy.
Bridging the Golden Gate.

Bibliography: p.
Includes index.
Summary: Details the story of the building of the bridge across the entrance to San Francisco Bay, once the longest and tallest bridge, but still beautiful and famous.
1. Golden Gate Bridge (San Francisco, Calif.)—Juvenile literature. [1. Golden Gate Bridge (San Francisco, Calif.)]
I. Title.
TG25.S225P45 1987 624′.55′097946 86-21077
ISBN 0-8225-1707-8 (lib. bdg.)
ISBN 0-8225-9521-4 (pbk.)

1 2 3 4 5 6 7 8 9 10 97 96 95 94 93 92 91 90 89 88 87

INKSTER PUBLIC LIBRARY
2005 INKSTER ROAD
INKSTER, MICHIGAN 48141

Contents

The Golden Gate Bridge and San Francisco's skyline, seen from the Pacific Ocean side.

They Said It Couldn't Be Done

The Golden Gate Bridge on the coast of California marks the United States' gateway to the Pacific. To Asian refugees the span has become the nation's "west coast Statue of Liberty," a symbol of freedom and hope.

From most of San Francisco's forty-three hills you can see the Golden Gate Bridge—most of the time. Some days only the tops of the red-orange towers poke through the fog. In summer, a thick fog bank may hide the bridge completely. But even when you cannot see it, you know it is there. You hear its bleating foghorns. One warns ships away from the south tower. Another beckons them to safe passage between the towers.

The bridge over the Golden Gate is known the world over. Yet it almost did not get built. The problem was the Gate itself.

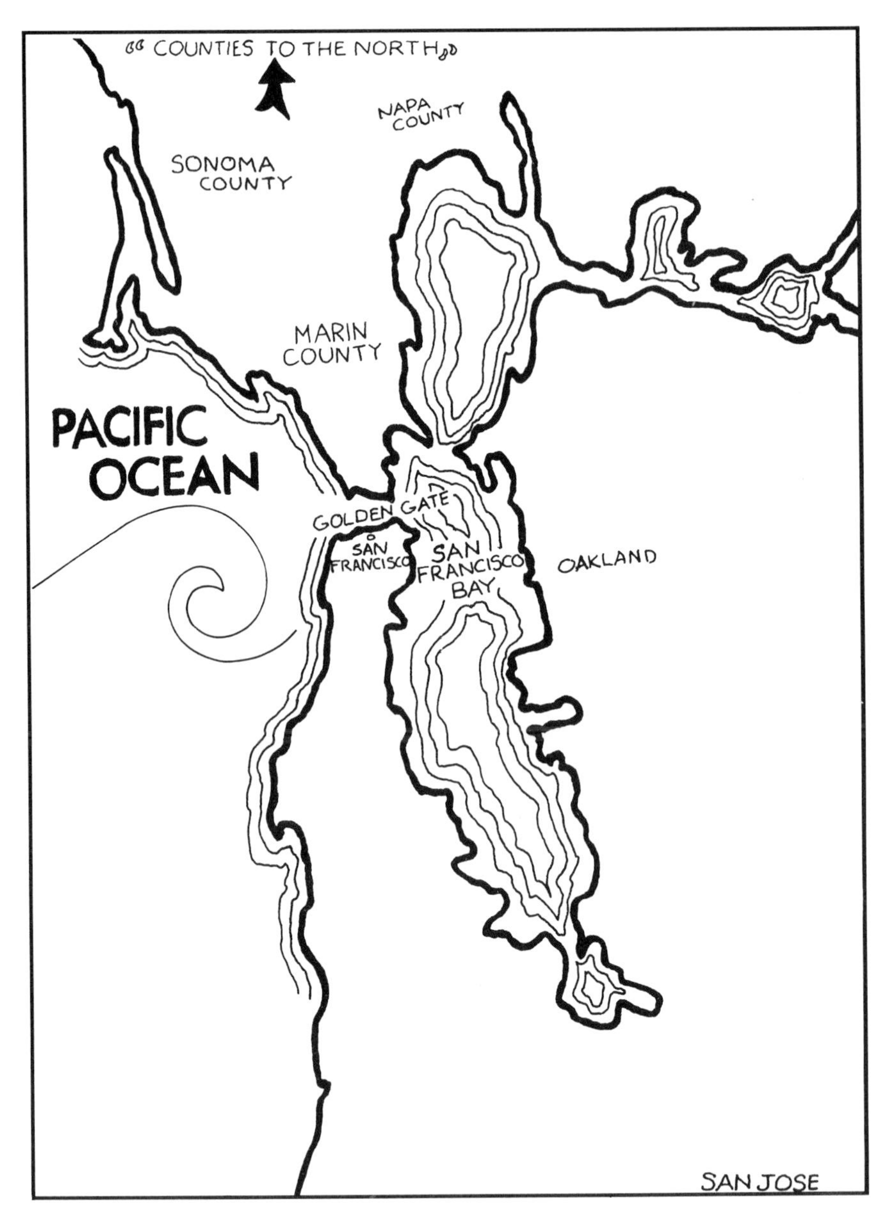

San Francisco is at the end of a peninsula. Before the Golden Gate was bridged, to go north from San Francisco people had to take the ferry across the Golden Gate or detour overland by way of San Jose to the south.

Even before there was a city of San Francisco, soldier and mapmaker John Charles Fremont gave the Golden Gate its name. To him it was that turbulent body of water between what is now San Francisco and the land to the north. Now some people call the bridge "the Golden Gate," when in fact that name refers to the channel under the bridge.

In the Golden Gate, the water is never still. Through this narrow entrance to San Francisco Bay, strong tides rush in twice each day and out twice each day.

For generations, there had been talk of bridging these treacherous waters. But no one took the talk seriously. How could anyone build a bridge over such a deep and wild channel? It would be impossible—or so people believed. Instead, those who wanted to cross the channel took a boat.

In the early 1800s, the only boats that regularly hauled passengers across this narrow, whitecapped strait were tank boats. San Francisco was still called Yerba Buena and it was a small village. In the summer the wells in the village ran dry. The tank boats brought water across the channel from the north. The boats ran with the tides. A passenger with enough money for the expensive ticket could ride along.

With the gold rush of 1849, sleepy Yerba Buena grew to be the bustling city of San Francisco. Gradually workers in the city began to spread out. They moved to the suburbs. Many went north of the Golden Gate to live in Marin County. After 1868, a regular ferry service across the Gate carried commuters to and from the city. Real estate salesmen began to promote "marvelous Marin." They urged other San Franciscans to discover the joys of country living. The Sausalito Land and Ferry Company even gave free passes on its sidewheeler ferry to all who bought lots in Sausalito, one of the towns to the north.

From time to time there was still talk in San Francisco

about bridging the Gate. In 1872, railroad owner Charles Crocker proposed a train bridge over the Golden Gate. Officials dismissed his scheme as "too daring," and people continued to ride the ferry.

The slow trip by ferry boat gave commuters time to visit with friends. They could eat a leisurely breakfast or dinner in the ferry's restaurant. But the unhurried pace did not suit everyone. It irritated newspaperman James Wilkins. In the *San Francisco Bulletin* of August 16, 1916, he wrote an article. He scoffed at talk that spanning those rough waters was too risky. The time had come, he argued, to "bridge the Gate!"

Some commuters loved the slow ferry ride. It gave them time to eat breakfast on the ferry while riding to work.

Old-fashioned ferry boats traveled the waters of the Golden Gate between Marin and San Francisco in half an hour. At the end of a holiday weekend there were long lines of traffic.

Wilkins, who was also a civil engineer, decided that a suspension bridge was needed. "It would be longer," he wrote, "than any other structure of its kind in the world."

James Wilkins's words created a stir on both sides of the Golden Gate. The county government of Marin, the Board of Supervisors, voted to begin a study of the idea immediately.

Could the Golden Gate really be bridged?

The newspaper campaign of James Wilkins interested a stranger in town. Joseph Baermann Strauss had come to San Francisco on business. Barely five feet tall, Strauss had always liked doing things bigger and better than anyone had done them before. Already he had built 400 bridges—in the United States, South America, Egypt, Russia, China, and Japan. Mr. Strauss was ambitious and stubborn, and the word "impossible" was not in his vocabulary. Creating the bridge that everyone said couldn't be built would be for him a challenge—his greatest challenge yet.

But by 1917 America was at war. This was not the time to talk of bridging the Golden Gate. Joseph Strauss did what he could to help the war effort. At forty-seven, he was too old to join the army, so he helped in other ways. He thought of many new ways of doing old things. He built concrete railroad cars to haul military supplies. He developed a portable searchlight for antiaircraft gunners. But for the duration of World War I, the bridge had to remain his dream.

Mr. Strauss continued to build other bridges. One day, when he was talking with San Francisco City Engineer M. M. O'Shaughnessy about another project, the conversation turned to Strauss's favorite subject—bridging the Golden Gate.

"Everybody says it can't be done," said O'Shaughnessy.

By now Joseph Strauss was familiar with the Golden Gate. He had studied it from the bluff overlooking Fort Point, an old fortress on the south shore. He had scrambled down the rocky path to the edge of the churning waters. He had heard waves crash against the breakwater and felt the force of ocean winds. He agreed with the city engineer that spanning the waters of the Golden Gate would be difficult.

Standing on the bridge under construction, Joseph Strauss, right, *spoke to an army officer. Some of the strongest opposition to the bridge came from the army, since the approach roads to the bridge had to pass through military land.*

"And even if it could be done," O'Shaughnessy continued, "it would cost over one hundred million dollars."

The small man looked at the city engineer towering above him.

"I believe I can do it," said Joseph Strauss, "and for far less."

To find out if bedrock near the Marin County shore was solid enough to support the north pier, geologists cut samples of rock from the bottom of the channel.

“Bridge the Gate!”

The San Francisco supervisors met on November 12, 1918, the day after the armistice ending World War I was signed. They ordered a study of the bridge site. During the month of February, 1920, a crew of geologists on the USS *Natoma* fought the rough waters of the channel to make soundings. They measured water depths between Fort Point on the south shore and Lime Point on the north.

San Francisco newspapers reported the geologists' findings: "Federal experts believe it will be impossible to put piers at this point, owing to strong currents and great depth."

There was that word again: Impossible! But it didn't bother Joseph Strauss.

For the next year he studied the geologists' survey and made calculations. He and his staff considered the weight the bridge would have to bear and whether bedrock on the channel bottom was solid enough to support that much weight. They figured where to sink the foundations for the bridge.

Four times each day strong tides rush in and out through the narrow channel of the Golden Gate between San Francisco and Marin.

On June 28, 1921, Mr. Strauss submitted his finished plan. Nothing happened. City officials were slow to act on it. Then some San Franciscans spoke out. They did not want a man-made bridge spoiling the natural beauty of their beloved Golden Gate. "It would be a blot on nature," they said.

Joseph Strauss was sensitive to the spectacular setting of his bridge. He did not want to spoil the bay landscape, but he wanted to build that bridge.

He knew he would have to have more support.

"The value of an idea," Strauss said, "depends not only on the sweat you put into thinking it up, but also on the sweat you put into getting people to accept it."

So he traveled across the Golden Gate to get support from people in the north, who were more eager to have a bridge. He spoke to businessmen and civic leaders, to ordinary people and politicians. Mr. Strauss told his listeners a bridge would bring prosperity. It would boost land values. It could shorten the time farmers spent hauling fruits and vegetables to market in the city.

He worked hard to convince the citizens of the north counties.

Finally, in 1923, the "Bridging the Golden Gate Association" formed. The Association convinced California lawmakers to form a district to finance a bridge. This Bridge District included San Francisco and the five counties or parts of counties to the north that wanted the bridge.

Then officials from the War Department stepped in.

"You would be building the bridge on land owned by the War Department," they said. "You can't do that without our approval."

An army colonel held hearings for seven months, while worried military officers voiced objections and Joseph Strauss defended his bridge.

"What if a ship hits your bridge?" one person asked.

"There will be four thousand feet between the piers," Strauss replied. "More than enough room for a deep shipping lane."

"If the bridge were hit by a bomb in a war," insisted another, "it would clog the harbor entrance. No ship could enter or leave."

Joseph Strauss glared at the officer. "If the enemy got so close as to be able to bomb the bridge, there would be very little left of the city."

The army hearings dragged on. But at last the secretary of war approved the bridge.

During those months, people began to take sides in the debate. In favor of the bridge were those in the north who felt the value of their property would go up if a bridge linked the north counties with San Francisco. Car dealers, too, were in favor. They felt they would sell more cars.

But many people were opposed to a bridge, so a superior court judge was assigned to travel from county to county to hear their arguments.

The ferry companies complained they would lose customers—and income. Environmentalists didn't want highways and traffic that might destroy the natural beauty of Marin County. Lumber companies did not want hordes of tourists interfering with their business in the majestic redwood forests.

"If it's too easy for folks to drive north," one farmer protested, "they'll turn my pasture into a picnic ground. They'll scare my cows."

The people of San Francisco had another worry. They remembered the big quake of 1906. What would happen, they asked, if the bridge were struck by an earthquake?

Joseph Strauss reassured them. His bridge could withstand a big earthquake, and hurricane winds of 100 miles an hour besides.

The hearings continued for many months. But finally, in December 1928, the judge ruled that the bridge could be built. Someone would have to manage the bridge, so directors for the Bridge District were selected from San Francisco and the five other counties to the north.

Joseph Strauss competed with ten other men for the job of chief engineer of the bridge. Strauss was selected. He asked his two closest rivals to join him as consulting engineers.

It had been eight years since Mr. Strauss handed his first bridge design to San Francisco's city engineer. The long delay turned out to be fortunate for him. It had given him time to build other bridges and learn more about building with steel. In 1921 his plan had been to use rigid braces at each end of the bridge. In the final plan, Joseph Strauss and his chief assistant, Clifford Paine, designed an all-suspension bridge with a center span four-fifths of a mile long. It would not need rigid supports to make it both strong and flexible. It would be able to swing with changes in temperature or when buffeted by Pacific storms.

Army officers demanded another hearing after the original design was changed. They feared there would not be enough clearance under the bridge for tall-masted vessels. The fact that the distance between bridge and water could vary by as much as sixteen feet confused the officers.

Patiently, Joseph Strauss told them about high and low tides. He explained that the cables would lengthen on hot days and shrink on cold days.

In his first design, in 1921, Joseph Strauss combined features of both cantilever *and* suspension *bridges. In a cantilever bridge, one end is solidly anchored to the land in order to support the part extending over the water. In a suspension bridge, the deck hangs by* suspenders *from cables which pass over two towers.*

"Oh," someone joked, "so you are building a rubber bridge?"

People laughed, but to Joseph Strauss building the bridge was a serious project. Eventually, he managed to persuade the War Department to approve his new design.

His next major difficulty was finding a way to finance the construction. It wasn't enough that the weary campaigner had spent a dozen years convincing people on both sides of the Golden Gate that a bridge was needed and he was the one to build it. Now he had to somehow raise the $35 million he would need to do the job.

The bridge would not be paid for with state or federal funds. One way governments and big companies borrow money is through the sale of bonds. The Bridge District could sell bonds publicly to finance the bridge. Over time the district could pay back the loan, or the bonds, with money from bridge tolls once the bridge was open. First, however, voters had to approve this way of raising money for the bridge.

Mr. Strauss knew that unhappy ferry patrons might be willing to pay for a bridge. After most holiday weekends the lines of cars waiting for ferries back to San Francisco stretched for seven to ten miles.

Voting to raise money for the bridge brought up the old arguments about safety and about loss of income for the ferries. It created a new worry, too: if construction costs turned out to be greater than Mr. Strauss's estimate, would the citizens be taxed to pay for the difference?

The "Taxpayers' Committee Against the Golden Gate Bridge Bonds" passed out leaflets. They claimed that $35 million would not begin to pay for the bridge and that the additional money needed would come from higher taxes. Members of the committee called the bridge "an outrage," a "wildcat scheme." Speakers lectured and took to the radio to claim the bridge would "mar the natural beauty of San Francisco's world-famed harbor entrance." Activists walked from house to house telling people to "vote NO on the bridge." Even Strauss's old friend, City Engineer O'Shaughnessy, was now against the idea. He signed a petition against the bridge.

Supporters fought back. They formed booster clubs, like the "Marvelous Marin, Inc." They handed out "Bridge the Gate" bumper stickers. On 20,000 car windshields, members of the Lions Club of San Anselmo plastered stickers that said "Why Wait? Bridge the Gate."

By 1930 the country had plunged into the Great Depression. Millions of people were out of work. The president of the San Francisco Chamber of Commerce declared that building the bridge could solve the local unemployment problem.

"It's the job of every voter in the city," he declared, "to create jobs by voting for the bridge."

The Bridge District promised to hire only laborers who had lived in one of the district's six counties for at least a year. It wanted jobs to go to local people.

In addition, Joseph Strauss gave his word to anxious taxpayers. No work would be done on the bridge if bids for construction costs went above $35 million.

Joseph Strauss waited. Would his promise to limit the costs of construction, and the district's promise of jobs, be enough to swing the vote in his favor?

He had fought the ferry operators, the lumber companies, the politicians, and the so-called experts who said the bridge could not and should not be built. But Strauss had always counted on the people to back him. If they didn't this time, his bridge would not be built.

Poet, dreamer, and master bridge builder Joseph Strauss spent a dozen years convincing people the Golden Gate could and should be bridged.

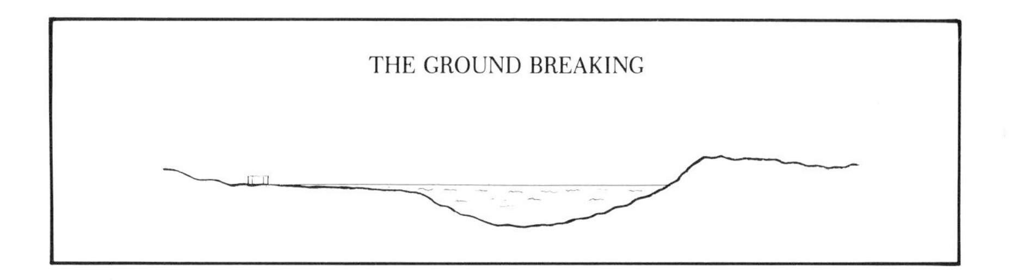

"Don't Be Afraid to Dream..."

It was a great victory for Joseph Strauss when the people on both sides of the Golden Gate voted three to one in favor of the bridge. They wanted that bridge! Storekeepers in Marin County closed early the day after the vote to celebrate. There was a parade with floats and fireworks. There were games, an air circus with stunt pilots, and a great bonfire in front of the Sonoma County Courthouse.

But still the opponents of the bridge refused to give up. Almost as soon as the ballots were counted, people began hinting that the engineering data had been "doctored." Geologists again had to brave the rough waters of the Golden Gate to prove that the channel bottom was solid bedrock.

A lawsuit was filed by a ferry company and the large railroad which owned it. They sued the Bridge District claiming it had been created illegally. When they lost their lawsuit, they threatened to appeal—to go to the Supreme Court, if necessary.

That would delay construction for months, or even years. Now the pro-bridge forces lectured and pleaded their case on the radio. They told people what had happened. Car dealers boycotted the railroad company, refusing to accept new cars shipped on its trains. Angry citizens forced the railroad to withdraw its appeal.

Now that the people had approved selling bonds to finance the bridge, a final, serious hurdle remained. Joseph Strauss had to find a bank that would guarantee that all the bonds would be bought, and would arrange for their resale to the public and to other bankers. He had to find a bank that had enough money to guarantee such a large purchase. Mr. Strauss appealed to A.P. Giannini, founder of the bank which later became Bank of America. Mr. Giannini pledged his bank's support.

"San Francisco needs that bridge," he said. "We'll take the bonds."

Now, work could begin.

The Bridge District asked for bids. Contracts were let for a company to put in concrete anchorages and piers, for steel experts to build the twin towers and the roadway, for a company to spin the giant cables, and finally, for builders to put in the approach roads at both ends of the finished bridge.

The official start of construction was January 5, 1933. It was an event to celebrate, and that's just what the people did. On February 26, 1933, a parade set out from the center of the city for the formal ground-breaking ceremony at the

NUMBER

1933-1983

United States of America

STATE OF CALIFORNIA

GOLDEN GATE BRIDGE AND HIGHWAY DISTRICT

BRIDGE BOND, SERIES B

1000

The Golden Gate Bridge and Highway District, a bridge and highway district duly organized and existing under the constitution and laws of the State of California, hereby acknowledges itself indebted and for value received promises to pay to the bearer, or if this bond be registered, to the registered owner hereof, on the 1st day of July, 1953, the principal sum of

ONE THOUSAND DOLLARS ($1,000.00)

together with interest thereon at the rate of 4¾ per centum per annum, payable semi annually on the first days of January and July of each year upon the presentation and surrender of the annexed interest coupons as they severally become due. Both principal and interest hereof are payable in lawful money of the United States at the office of Bank of America National Trust and Savings Association, San Francisco, California, or at the Manufacturers Trust Company, in the City of New York, at the option of the holder. For the prompt payment hereof, both principal and interest as the same become due, the full faith and credit of said District are hereby irrevocably pledged.

This bond is one of a series issued by said District for the purpose of constructing a public toll bridge across the Golden Gate with approaches, connecting roads and appurtenances, under the authority of and in full compliance with an act of the legislature of the State of California entitled, "An act to provide for the incorporation and organization and management of bridge and highway districts and to provide for the acquisition and construction by said districts of highways, bridges and approaches thereto, and for the acquisition of all property necessary therefor and also to provide for the issuance and payment of bonds by said districts, for the levying of taxes and the collection of tolls by said districts, and for the annexation of additional territory thereto," approved May 25, 1923, and acts supplemental thereto and amendatory thereof, and pursuant to a vote of more than two thirds of the electors of said District voting at an election legally called and held and resolutions duly adopted by the Board of Directors of said District.

It is hereby certified and recited that all acts, conditions and things required to happen, exist and be performed precedent to and in the issuance of this bond, have happened, exist and have been performed in due time, form and manner as required by the laws and Constitution of California; that the total indebtedness of said District, including this bond, does not exceed any constitutional or statutory limitation thereon; and that provision has been made by law for the levy and collection of a direct annual tax upon all taxable property within said District sufficient to pay the principal and interest of this bond.

This bond is subject to registration as to principal thereof and also as to both principal and interest in accordance with provisions endorsed hereon.

In Witness Whereof, said Golden Gate Bridge and Highway District has caused this bond to be signed by the President and countersigned by the Secretary of Board of Directors, and the official seal of said District to [illegible] hereto [illegible] fixed, and the annexed interest coupons to be [illegible] with [illegible] facsimile signatures of said officers, and this bond [illegible] dated the first day of July, 1933.

1000

To get money to build the Golden Gate Bridge, bonds like this were sold. Bond holders were repaid their purchase price, plus interest, from bridge toll money.

San Francisco bridgehead. Uniformed school bands tooted trumpets and trombones and tubas to lead the way. Thousands joined the march. The joyful crowd swarmed so close to the speakers' platform they nearly knocked it over. They cheered as an official read President Herbert Hoover's telegram of congratulations. Overhead, navy planes flew in formation. Skywriters sketched a smoky outline of a bridge in the sky. Engineering students from the University of California at Berkeley unveiled the eighty-foot model of the bridge they had built. The model was nearly bent in half as 100,000 enthusiastic citizens surged by.

San Francisco's Mayor Rossi pushed his gold spade into the ground to turn over the first clump of dirt. People shouted their approval. Another cheer went up as 250 carrier pigeons flew from their cages to speed the message to the corners of the state: construction on the bridge had begun at last.

It had taken Joseph Strauss a long time to reach this moment. It would take him another four years, he estimated, to build his bridge. But build it he would!

"Our world of today," he said, "revolves completely around things which at one time couldn't be done because they were supposedly beyond the limits of human endeavor. Don't be afraid to dream."

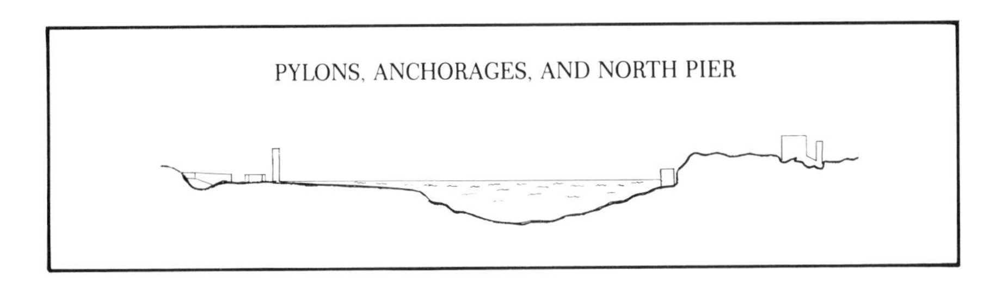

"Eight for Eight, or Out the Gate"

A crowd of jobless workers gathered behind the fence at a construction site on the San Francisco bridgehead. The leather soles of the shoes on most of the men were worn thin from weeks of walking the streets looking for work.

The crew foreman at the site pointed to one of the men in the crowd.

"You!" barked the foreman.

The man grinned. He left the others waiting at the fence. But he didn't walk to his new job—he ran.

During the Great Depression of the 1930s, people all across the country were out of work. In the San Francisco area, one in four workers was unemployed. It is no wonder that the Golden Gate Bridge project offered hope. The promise of work was the best thing that happened to the jobless in the Bridge District. Experts predicted that the bridge would provide 25 million man-hours of work, and 3 million days of labor. To a man without a job, those fancy words simply meant that if he hung around the construction area long enough he might—like so many others—be hired.

The rule on the Golden Gate Bridge project was "eight for eight, or out the gate!" Foremen were quick to fire anyone who didn't put eight hours' worth of work in an eight-hour day. There were always plenty of others waiting for the job. Though it was depression time, a laborer could earn $5.50 a day. That was not bad, considering that in those days a person could rent a five-room house for $30 a month, or buy three heads of lettuce for a nickel.

The Bridge District kept its promise to hire local laborers only. On the radio you could hear officials discouraging the jobless from coming out west.

"Don't come to San Francisco in search of work," they said. "It's useless."

Of course, some people tried to get jobs though they had not lived in the area long enough to qualify. A few tried to cheat to get past the residency rule. They changed dates on gas or water bills. Or they bribed a landlord to lie about how long the newcomer had lived at the rooming house.

The men who were hired for bridge jobs had to work hard to keep those jobs. The project needed not only bridge workers, but also workers in mills, mines, and quarries. Drivers were needed to haul materials. Road crews with shovels and road graders were hired to build roads for getting men and equipment to the work site. Joseph Strauss even built his own cement manufacturing plant to be sure he would get the kind of cement he needed.

There were many jobs for truck drivers. The Golden Gate Bridge project was the first to use mixer trucks which mixed the concrete as they drove to the work site.

Even before the official ground breaking in February of 1933, giant steam shovels had begun to dig the two pits for the north anchorages. Each pit was so deep a ten-story building could fit easily inside. But it was concrete, not a building, that was going into each eighty-foot pit. As soon as carpenters built the wooden forms in them, mixer trucks poured in a layer of concrete. Carpenters waited for the layer to harden, then built another set of forms so another layer could be poured.

Carpenters built wooden forms to give shape to poured concrete. Steel reinforcing rods were set in the concrete to make it strong. This massive structure would be a bridge support, called a pylon.

Afterward, carpenter's helpers removed the forms and took out the nails so the wood could be used over again.

Large steel loops, called *eyebars*, were embedded in the concrete. Later the cables would be fastened to these eyebars. Since the cables would hold up the roadway, the strain on the anchorages would be tremendous.

The anchorages on the San Francisco side of the channel took longer to build. Historic Fort Point, a relic of the Civil War era, stood in the way. Crews had to build a protective arch over it.

The powdery cement for the concrete was manufactured from crushed oyster shells at a plant twenty-five miles to the south. Barges brought the dry cement to *batching plants* built near construction sites on both sides of the Golden Gate. The cement was stored in silos until needed. Then it was *batched*, or combined with water and fine gravel to make concrete. The concrete was poured into trucks, which mixed it as they drove to the work sites.

Through the spring of 1933, crews continued work on the anchorages while another crew began to build the north pier. The piers would be the foundations rising from the channel floor to support the twin towers. The site for the north pier was in shallow water at the base of a cliff. To provide a dry place to build the north pier, engineers constructed a circular wall next to the cliff. This was called a *cofferdam*. They pumped out all the water. Inside the dry cofferdam, workers began to dig into the bedrock.

With dynamite and jackhammers and a steam shovel, crews blasted and carved a hole longer and wider than a football field. As with the anchorages, carpenters built a

Ocean waves lapped onto the rocky shore on the San Francisco side of the Golden Gate near Fort Point, where the anchorages were built. Later, the cables were attached to these huge concrete anchorages.

A circular wall called a cofferdam *was built around the site of the north pier so men would have a dry place to work. The north pier was built close to shore, next to a steep cliff in Marin County. The wooden structure in the foreground is the Lime Point lighthouse.*

network of wooden forms for pouring concrete. Then, mixer trucks brought the concrete, chuting it down through a large funnel called an *elephant trunk*. Below, men in rubber boots jumped on the wet concrete, moving it around so that the area was evenly covered.

When the north pier was finished, it rose higher than a six-story building. It weighed 45,000 tons.

Unfortunately, Joseph Strauss had worked so hard during his long campaign to convince the people to build the bridge that he had had a nervous breakdown. He had been forced to take a rest. This meant he had missed the first three months of construction of the anchorages and north pier.

When Joseph Strauss came back, he and Clifford Paine turned their attention elsewhere. The time had come to build the more difficult south pier. All along they had known that this would be their greatest challenge.

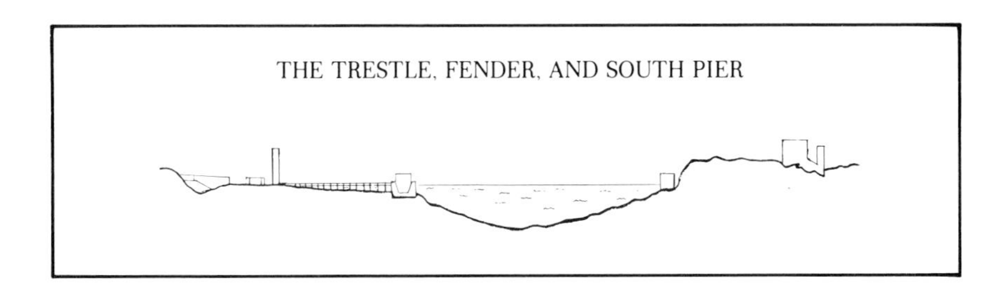

THE TRESTLE, FENDER, AND SOUTH PIER

"The Giant Bathtub"

Joseph Strauss stood on the San Francisco shore of the Golden Gate. He studied the wind-whipped channel. A quarter of a mile offshore, under sixty-five feet of water, was the sloping ledge where he must erect the south pier. Working so far from shore, his crews would have no protection from wind and waves.

Earlier, when geologists surveyed the channel, rough seas had forced them to stop work for days at a time. Their exploration barge had pitched and rolled. Often the men had become seasick. It would be the same for the men trying to put in the south pier.

Joseph Strauss and Clifford Paine had already decided to build a circle of concrete around the work site. This concrete *fender-ring* would have walls thick as a house. It would shield workers from the full force of ocean storms and strong winds. Later, the fender would keep the pier and tower from being struck by ships and floating objects.

Excavating the fender site would have to be done from a barge. But building the fender itself from a wave-tossed barge was out of the question. Instead, the chief engineer and his assistant designed a trestle, like a long wooden dock extending out to the work site. Over it they would run telephone and electricity lines, compressed air hoses, and water pipes. The trestle would be strong enough to support trucks and other heavy equipment.

A crew began work on the trestle in February of 1933. By late that summer, it was nearly finished.

The wind stirred up whitecaps near the trestle. The dredger bobbed up and down as much as eight feet as it loaded a refuse barge with debris from the channel bottom a hundred feet below. On the south shore, the mighty pylons were ready to support the end of the bridge.

Then, on August 14, disaster struck.

It was one of those damp, gray, San Francisco days. A thick summer fog covered the bay. A freighter heading out to sea veered off course. Despite warnings from the foghorns, the freighter charged ahead. It smashed through the trestle's midsection with a thunderous crash, slicing the wooden dock in half.

It was a terrible setback. Repairs to the trestle cost $10,000. Work on the project was delayed for three months. But finally, by late October, crews had rebuilt the trestle and were ready to start on the fender.

Then, on Halloween night, winds began to howl and another disaster struck. A fierce Pacific storm developed. Violent waves lashed at the trestle. Before morning the waves had smashed almost the whole dock into the channel. Another storm a few days later finished the job.

Years before, when Joseph Strauss first proposed spanning the Golden Gate, everyone had said, "Impossible! You can never build a bridge foundation in the open sea."

Were the people right, after all?

Strauss and Paine decided that whatever the cost, they had to rebuild the trestle. It meant another $100,000 and another delay—five months this time. But it was a good decision.

Through the winter of 1933 a new and stronger trestle went up. By April of 1934, the crew was ready at last to put in the fender.

Earlier, when men had blasted the bedrock to build the north pier, they worked in the dry cofferdam. But to excavate the site for the fender, which was the first step in building the south pier, the crew had to work from a barge. They depended on help from marine divers to blast the channel bedrock.

The divers who worked on the channel bottom during the building of the south fender and pier had dangerous jobs. Their heavy helmets, belts of lead weights, and iron sandals helped keep them from bobbing back up when they touched bottom.

The excavation crew worked from the barge *Ajax*. The barge often pitched up and down as much as eight feet on the waves. The men sent explosives down through a steel tube. They dropped six slender *bombs* at a time—each loaded with 200 pounds of dynamite. When all six were in place, divers connected wires to them. Then the *Ajax* crew quickly hoisted the divers, moved out of range, and set off the charges.

Each blast ripped a fifteen-foot hole in the bedrock. The surface of the water barely rippled.

Men operating dredgers scooped up the broken rock and dumped it in barges. By the time the refuse barges finished their job, they had hauled off enough debris to fill a football stadium.

Before concrete was poured for the fender, divers worked to smooth the channel bottom. Like undersea fire fighters, they wrestled huge hoses that shot water under 500 pounds of pressure to clean out the rough corners of the excavation site.

The divers could only work for twenty minutes at a time, during the four slack periods each day at low and high tides. In each short space of time they had to finish their job, then come up quickly.

Sometimes a diver shot up too quickly, without enough time to decompress. "Tender!" someone would yell. "Get him to the chamber—before he gets the bends!"

Helpers would yank off the diver's heavy helmet and bundle him into a waiting pickup which would tear back along the trestle to the decompression chamber on shore. The diver was put in the chamber, where pressure was immediately increased until it was the same as the pressure at the depth where the diver had been working. Then the pressure in the chamber was gradually decreased. This let the diver "come up" to surface pressure again, but more slowly. It gave nitrogen bubbles present in the diver's blood time to dissolve. Otherwise, the nitrogen bubbles would leave the bloodstream and come out into the joints, causing a painful and serious condition known as the *bends*.

The divers came from Washington and Oregon. Workers with special skills, such as the divers, did not have to be residents. The men who undertook this dangerous job had worked in the swirling waters of the Columbia River. They were used to working fast and doing most of their tasks in the murky water by feel.

The plan for building the fender was to form solid concrete blocks on the channel floor. Block by block, the crew would build up the fender as one makes a brick wall.

A *derrick crane* was brought to the end of the trestle. A derrick is a device used in construction jobs to lift and move heavy objects. The derrick crane lowered steel *guide frames* to the channel bottom. Divers guided the huge frames into place. These frames formed the box into which the concrete would be poured. If two steel frames didn't fit together tightly enough, the divers patched the open spaces with wire mesh to prevent concrete from oozing out.

When the steel frames were in place, mixer trucks brought in the concrete. They poured *hydraulic concrete*, which will set under water. It was chuted through a long metal funnel called a *tremie pipe*. As the concrete level rose, the tremie pipe was slowly raised so the end of the pipe wasn't buried in the concrete.

Soon a thick concrete wall appeared above the surface of the water. "It's starting to look like a giant bathtub," someone suggested.

More concrete was poured. Now the fender rose thirty-four feet above the water.

As mixer trucks delivered loads of concrete, the fender grew, block by block. When finished, the fender contained 146,000 tons of concrete.

One end of the fender was left open, so the fender was shaped like a giant horseshoe. Through the open space, Joseph Strauss would float in a huge, steel, bottomless box. Then the gap would be closed, and the box sunk and pumped dry. The box was called a *caisson*. Inside the caisson, crews would have a protected place to work on the channel floor while they poured concrete for the south pier. The caisson would remain in place, becoming a part of the pier.

Unfortunately, things didn't work out as Joseph Strauss planned.

The October morning when the caisson was floated inside the fender and moored, the sea was calm and the breeze gentle. It was planned that, for the next two weeks, crews would pour concrete blocks to close the gap in the fender. Then the caisson could be sunk. But the night the caisson was moored, the wind picked up. The sea became choppy. At nine o'clock Joseph Strauss was summoned by phone.

"The caisson!" croaked the night watchman's scared voice. "It's rocking. It'll break its lines in that wind."

Strauss rushed to the trestle. Inside the fender, the rocking and pitching caisson strained at its mooring lines. If the heavy steel caisson broke loose, it would be like a battering ram. It could ruin the fender.

"Divers went down...," a voice shouted, "...a few hours ago....tried to put in anchoring posts...didn't help."

Joseph Strauss hesitated. He had counted on using the caisson. Without it, he and his contractor would have to develop a new procedure for building the south pier. The time and money spent on the caisson thus far would be lost. But he couldn't allow the caisson to damage the fender. What if another storm came up during those two weeks when the gap was being closed? The caisson, trapped inside, could batter the fender to pieces. That would mean the loss of even more time and money. It could endanger the entire project.

Joseph Strauss had to make his decision soon. Should he cut the caisson loose, or leave it in place—at the risk of having it destroy the entire fender? At midnight, he gave the order.

"Let the caisson go," he snapped.

Hurried instructions went to the two divers: "Go down. Free its anchors!"

The divers slid into the turbulent waters. They rigged extra lines, which they could tug to get help from "upstairs" if they were slammed against the caisson.

Feeling their way in the pitch-black water, the divers together struggled to loosen the big pins that held the caisson's lines. They bent the pins back and forth, working the metal. Finally they pulled out the pins and came to the surface.

"Of all the experience I had as a diver," one of them admitted afterward, "I used the bulk of it right there on that dive."

The useless caisson was towed away before it could wreck the fender.

"Looks like Mother Nature pulled the plug on Mr. Strauss's giant bathtub," said the jokesters. But to Joseph Strauss it was no joke. It was a real disaster. He had intended to use the caisson as a form for pouring concrete for the pier. Now he would have to build the south pier another way. As soon as the missing blocks of the concrete bathtub were filled in, he would have to pump out the water. The dry fender would be like the cofferdam that was built around the site of the north pier.

The missing concrete blocks were poured and the fender was finished. Immediately the water inside it became calm.

Inside the "giant bathtub" all was calm. The thirty-foot-thick fender ring, a quarter-mile offshore, kept out ocean waves and wind. As soon as the ring was pumped dry, workers poured concrete for the south pier.

Divers went down to explore. They found hundreds of trapped devilfish, cod, small sharks, jellyfish—even an octopus.

"The giant bathtub," they shouted, "is now the world's biggest fishbowl!"

Millions of gallons of water were pumped from the fender, leaving the fish on the bottom.

"Fish fry tonight!" one worker yelled as he and the others began scooping up their "catch."

It was January 1935. The worst was over. A determined Joseph Strauss had won—over the nay-sayers, and over the full fury of nature. The giant bathtub-turned-fishbowl was now dry. Finally, construction of the south pier could begin.

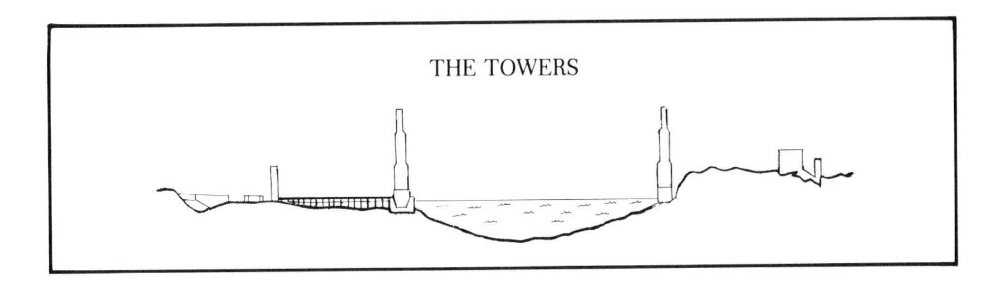

"Walking the Beam"

Because steel contracts when it is cold and expands when it is hot, engineers must consider temperature when they design a bridge. For example, a bridge built in Alaska and moved to the tropics would grow longer because the steel would expand due to the heat. If the bridge measured 700 feet when temperatures dropped to forty-five degrees below zero, that same bridge would measure 700 feet and 9 inches when the temperature soared to one hundred twenty degrees.

At the Golden Gate, temperatures never reach those extremes, but the engineers still had to allow for a considerable range.

Engineers designing a bridge must also figure how much weight the bridge can support and how much wind it can withstand. The towers on a suspension bridge support the cables. The cables, in turn, hold up the roadway and all of the traffic load—on windy days, as well as calm. Since each tower bears half the total weight, each tower needs to be strong and flexible.

Long before Joseph Strauss's engineers built the first tower for the Golden Gate Bridge, they tested a thirteen-foot steel model of it. They simulated traffic loads and temperature changes. They calculated how much a full-size tower could safely bend when the steel cables it supported expanded or contracted. The engineers placed their model in a wind tunnel that simulated the winds that howl through the Golden Gate, to test how the full-size tower would react.

The twin towers on the Golden Gate Bridge would not be solid columns of steel. Instead, they would be built of hundreds of small steel boxes, riveted together. These boxes, or *cells*, had the floor size of a telephone booth—about a yard on a side—but they were thirty-five feet high. The cells were made at a steel plant in Pennsylvania. Holes were drilled where rivets would be set to connect one cell to another. These prefabricated cells were shipped to California by way of the Panama Canal and then stored at a warehouse on the east side of San Francisco Bay.

Work was due to begin on the north tower in the summer of 1933. But first, the pier on which the tower would stand had to be smoothed. Workers used a grinding wheel to grind smooth the surface of the concrete pier. They had to work so exactly that any bump greater than 1/32 inch—the thickness of a dime—had to be scraped down. Then a cement of red lead paste was spread over the surface and thick steel base plates were set in place. The tower legs would rest on these steel plates. Holes 6½ inches in diameter had been predrilled in both the steel plates and the concrete surface of the pier. Steel dowels driven through the holes secured the base plates.

The steel contractor in charge of building the towers hired only experienced bridgemen, who came from all parts of the country. Again, in order to get workers with special skills, Joseph Strauss waived the residency requirement. But he still hired both skilled and unskilled local laborers to help.

The bridgemen, sometimes called bridge monkeys or ironmen, were able to skitter along narrow steel girders hundreds of feet in the air. "Walking the beam," they called it. These nimble workers could climb up steel walls by stepping on rows of rivets.

Construction of the north tower began in late summer of 1933, while crews on the south side were still trying to build the trestle out to the work site.

Barges hauled the sixty-five-ton steel cells, a few at a time, from the storage yard to the north pier. The huge steel boxes were hoisted onto the pier. To set them in place, crews used a special derrick with two booms—one for each leg of the tower.

A crew of *bolter-ups* matched the predrilled holes to fit the cells. Riveters working in the cramped cells riveted the steel pieces together. The cells were dark inside, and echoed with the constant din of the riveting gun. When the light in a riveter's hat went out, which it often did, he couldn't see what he was doing. Besides everything else, the air smelled bad in the stuffy cells when hot rivets melted the protective paint on the steel.

At noon, riveting gangs grabbed their lunch pails and headed for fresh air.

The riveting teams included *heaters*, who heated the rivets, and *bucker-ups* and *riveters*, who set them. The heater worked over a fire in a black iron tub, cooking rivets the size of hot dogs. It was like tending a barbecue grill. Each rivet was a steel bar with a rounded head at one end of the shank. The heater shot the white-hot rivets to the

Traveler derricks *could lift themselves higher as the legs of the tower got taller. By 1935 the south tower was started and the north tower was finished.*

rest of his team through a pneumatic tube. Air pressure forced the rivet around and up and down through the cells until it landed in a wire mesh trap where it was needed. The bucker-up snatched up the hot rivet with pliers and backed it, shank end first, into the proper hole that was matched to the hole in the cell next to it. As the bucker-up pressed on the rivet head with an iron bar, the riveter in the next cell pushed against the shank end with his air jackhammer to shape a second head. The rivet shrank lengthwise as it cooled so that both heads gripped the two walls, holding the two cells tightly together.

When a layer of cells had been set with rivets, the derrick with two booms crept up between the tower legs to the next level. As the tower grew, the members of a riveting team might be separated by a distance as great as half a city block. Each tower leg was a honeycomb of hundreds of cells, connected by small crawl holes and twenty-three miles of ladders.

"Although I designed this weird labyrinth," Joseph Strauss admitted, "I doubt if I could find my way out of it."

The route from top to bottom through the cells did not follow a straight line. There was even a twenty-six-page book of instructions to show the men how to get through the cells. There were tales of workers getting so badly lost they ended up spending the night in the tower.

The tower workers became adept at climbing through the maze because they were paid only for hours actually worked, not for the time they spent getting there. The fastest way was to climb the inside of the cell walls by stepping up the rows of rivet heads. "Like monkeys on the side of a palm tree," someone joked.

By the time the work places were high in the tower, the climb by ladder could take half an hour. Later they installed a block-and-tackle elevator the men called a *skip-box*. This made going up and down easier.

By March of 1934, when the north tower was nearly built, workers began to have strange complaints. Their breathing became shallow. Their hair and teeth started to fall out. What was this mysterious disease? At first, doctors suspected appendicitis. But soon there were sixty men with the same symptoms.

At last the mystery was solved. The men had lead poisoning. The bad smell of the hot rivets touching the paint was actually poisonous gas. The predrilled rivet holes had been treated with lead paint.

Immediately Joseph Strauss ordered several precautions. The steel company in Pennsylvania had to change the paint for the rest of the cells it shipped to California. Riveting gangs were given respirator masks to wear, and medicine to counter the effects of the lead. Fresh air was piped into the stuffy cells.

The precautions worked! There was no more sickness.

People on the north and south shores of the Golden Gate watched the progress of the north tower as it grew taller by the week.

On May 4, 1934, the last piece of steel had been hoisted and riveted. The north tower reached its full height: 746 feet above the water—twice as high as the tallest skyscraper in San Francisco. Jubilant workers raised the American flag in an informal ceremony at the top.

Eight months later, work on the south tower began. It was built the same way as its twin. This time the experienced crews worked faster. The pace was feverish to make up for months of work time lost building the trestle and the fender for the south pier.

The motto became: "Three hundred fifty a day or you're

Huge pylons to support the south side of the bridge were now 187 feet high. The traveler derrick had moved higher on the south tower.

out." Riveting teams that couldn't put in 350 rivets a day lost their jobs to riveting teams that could meet the quota.

Before the towers had cables and a roadway to steady them, they swayed in the wind. When they swayed a lot, the steelworkers on top of the towers lay on their stomachs, watching the skyline of San Francisco bob up and down.

One June morning the south tower began to move back and forth more than usual.

"What's happening?" someone yelled. "This tower's swinging like a hammock!"

Right: *Hundreds of steel boxes were riveted together to make each tower. The towers were made narrower at the top. At the base of each leg there were 103* cells, *or boxes. At the top, there were only 23. The spikes halfway up the tower later supported the sidewalk.* Below: *This photograph was taken from an airplane flying over San Francisco in March, 1935. Beyond the unfinished towers is the entrance to the Pacific Ocean. San Francisco Bay is this side of the towers.*

Workers on top of the tower began scuttling down ladders to lower cells. One man yanked on a pair of leather gloves, grabbed the greasy derrick cable, and slid down to the next level. By now the half dozen men who were still on top were throwing up. A man was trapped in the open-air elevator which was also beginning to swing, first away from the tower, then back into it with a bang. It was an earthquake.

There was another earthquake the next day. Fortunately, neither quake hurt the tower. The engineers were pleased that the flexible towers proved to be earthquake-proof. That would silence the doubters who had warned: "Just wait 'til there's an earthquake, *then* you'll see...."

"Without those millions of pounds of cables attached," Clifford Paine said, "the tower acted like a tuning fork. It vibrated." When the cables were attached, it would be stable.

By the summer of 1935, both towers were done. They contained 44,400 tons of steel and a total of 1.2 million rivets. Delighted residents of Napa County, forty miles to the north, reported seeing the towers. To the "shoreline superintendents"—people nearby who had watched from both shores for all those months—the two tall towers rising from the turbulent channel waters were proof enough. Mr. Strauss was on his way to bridging the Golden Gate at last!

It was a long walk up a catwalk between towers. Workers grabbed a moving rope for support while making the steep climb. Over their heads, the cable-spinning wheels were at work.

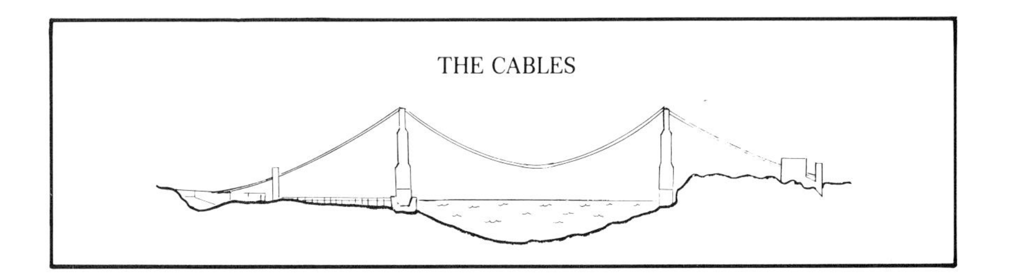

Spinners in the Air

Joseph Strauss chose John A. Roebling and Sons of New Jersey, builders of the Brooklyn Bridge, to spin the cables for the Golden Gate Bridge. He felt they were "the best in the business." The contract paid them nearly $6 million.

In earlier times, suspension bridge cables were assembled on land. Then derricks hoisted the cables onto the towers. But no derrick in the world could lift cables as heavy as the ones for the Golden Gate Bridge would be. The Roebling Company spun the cables in the air, on-site.

Roebling's carpenters built a work deck around the top of the Marin tower. Later, after the tower on the San Francisco side was finished, they built a work deck around it, too.

The steel saddles *provided a seat for the cables as they passed over the tower tops. An engineer in a hard hat was inspecting the spinning wheels in this picture, taken atop the south tower. San Francisco is in the background.*

With derricks, crews hoisted huge steel *saddles* to the tops of the towers. The spun cables would lie over these saddles.

The next step was to build footbridges across the Gate. On these *catwalks*, crews spinning the cables would be able to get from one side of the channel to the other.

On a foggy August morning in 1935, two Coast Guard boats closed the Golden Gate to all traffic. Ships and boats could not enter or leave until a guide rope for the catwalks was stretched across the Gate.

One end of a thick wire rope was tied to the Marin anchorage. A reel containing the rest of the rope was put on a barge. Two tugboats towed the barge slowly across the channel, unreeling 5,000 feet of the wire rope. When the barge reached the San Francisco side, the other end of the rope was tied to that anchorage.

Now the wire rope had to be hoisted 746 feet to the top of each tower. From work decks on the towers, men dropped lines to hook onto the wire rope and then brought it up. When they draped the rope over each tower, onlookers from the Marin and San Francisco shores could see the wet wire glisten. With the first rope as a guide, more were draped over the towers. Not quite like a bridge yet—but it was a start. The Gate was spanned!

Sightseers jammed cruise boats that sailed from San Francisco's waterfront for a firsthand look at the marvel.

Steel riggers had only two thin cables to hang onto as they constructed that first catwalk across the channel.

Roebling's crew adjusted the sag of each rope so it was exactly three feet below the path the cable would later follow.

When enough ropes were draped over the towers, carpenters added redwood planking to make catwalks. There were two catwalks—one on the ocean side of the towers, the other to the east, on the bay side. Now workers could walk above the water from one shore of the Golden Gate to the other for the first time.

The Roebling Company sent its experienced staff to supervise. They "hired and fired and hired and fired" local workers until they got the kind of cable-spinning crew they needed. They gave each man a week's training.

Above each catwalk were the wheels to spin the cables. Behind these workers on the east catwalk you can see the hills of San Francisco on an overcast fall day in 1935.

The spinning for each cable was done with a wheel that raced back and forth between the anchorages at a rate of 650 feet a minute, about 7½ miles per hour. The wire carried by the wheel was looped first onto a fixture at one anchorage, then onto one at the other. This wire was less than one-fifth of an inch thick—no thicker than a drinking straw. But when the spinning job was done, 55,054 of these thin wires would make up the two strong cables to support the roadway.

Some of the crew lubricated pulleys. Workers stood every fifty feet along each catwalk looking for snags and straightening out kinks in the wire. Helpers spliced wires between the end of one spool and the beginning of the next. A man's job might be to help electricians replace light bulbs. Many worked in the signal huts on the walkway. If a wire slipped off its trolley or some other problem developed, these men signaled a warning. They flashed lights, rang bells, sounded horns, or called by telephone, depending on who they were trying to signal, and where that person was—on the catwalk, at a saddle atop one of the towers, or at one of the anchorages.

Winter began at the same time as the spinning. Along the northern California coast it seldom rains in the summer. But in the winter it rains often, a cold wind blows from the Pacific Ocean, and there are many storms.

Cable-spinning stopped when it rained. But crews did not stop work when the wind blew, which it did most of the time. Workers standing along the catwalks had no protection from it. Even bundled in layers of sweaters and coats they felt numb. Their only chance to get away from the cold was when they could escape for a few minutes into one of the warm-up shacks along the catwalks.

Experts in the business not only taught the new workers how to spin cables, they offered them other advice, too.

This crew was strapping several hundred wires into a strand. *The galvanized iron warm-up shacks along each catwalk provided the only escape from the howling winds and freezing temperatures.*

"The trick in a big blow," said the old-timers, "is to lean into the wind, so it won't blow you clear over."

It was a good thing to know. In mid-December a forty-mile-an-hour gale swept through the Golden Gate. Catwalks swung back and forth eight feet. Yet work still continued as the wheels spun their wire strands.

When there were between 200 and 400 parallel wires, the wires were strapped together to form a *strand*. Sixty-one strands made up each thick cable. The strands were attached to the eyebars embedded in the concrete anchorages on both sides of the channel.

Workers placed bets on when the last wire would be spun. A timekeeper named Paul won the bet. His guess was off by only two minutes. The staff from Roebling and their helpers completed the spinning job on May 20, 1936, at 2:13 P.M. It had taken them six months and nine days. For the next two days, they celebrated.

So did Joseph Strauss. With cables for support, the roadway could now be built.

A special machine squeezed and compacted the sixty-one strands into a round cable. Later, wrapping machines wound a layer of fine wire around each cable.

Joseph Strauss's safety net under the deck was something new in bridge construction. The net, made of rope, was stretched on a steel frame below the area where the men were working and ten feet to either side of the roadway. During construction the net saved nineteen lives.

Safety First

During the first three and a half years of building the Golden Gate Bridge, not a single life had been lost. In the hazardous occupation of bridge building, that was unusual. Chief Engineer Strauss had reason to be pleased.

Since the days of London Bridge there had been a saying that "every bridge requires a life." In more recent times, bridge builders had turned the old saying into a formula: "One life for every million dollars worth of construction."

"An appalling sacrifice," Joseph Strauss called it. He vowed to prove the formula wrong. So far he had succeeded.

Part of the reason for his excellent safety record may have been luck. But luck wasn't all he depended upon. Being a practical man as well as a dreamer, Joseph Strauss did not leave things to chance. During construction he did what he could to make sure that accidents did not happen. He intended to keep his workers safe.

Joseph Strauss insisted that workers wear leather safety helmets. In the 1930s, they didn't have metal hard hats. Men who worked in dangerous places had to wear safety belts with a *tie-off line*—a length of rope tied from their belt to something secure.

When bridge monkeys tried to show off, Mr. Strauss was not impressed. Bridge building was dangerous under the best of conditions. "To the annoyance of the daredevils who loved to stunt at the end of the cables, far out in space," he said, "we fired any man we caught stunting on the job."

Joseph Strauss put up a field hospital near the work site, with a nurse on duty at all times. Hundreds of minor complaints and a few serious injuries from accidents were treated. Fortunately, the only serious health problem had been the lead poisoning. Since then Mr. Strauss had tried to make sure there would be no other. He insisted workers wash their hands often to prevent the spread of infections. He had special diets prescribed for steelworkers so they would not get dizzy at great heights. Anyone with a hangover had to take a big dose of sauerkraut juice. And any man caught drinking on the job was fired on the spot.

Men working on the tower were often above the fog. Sunlight reflecting off the white fog bank below them was like the glare of sun on white snow and it bothered their eyes. A doctor designed special, tinted, aviator goggles for the men, to keep them from getting *snow blindness*.

When it came time to build the roadway, Joseph Strauss and Clifford Paine were concerned because it was such a dangerous project. They knew the crews would have no catwalks to stand on. There would be no rope handrail for a worker to grab if he lost his balance or slipped on a slick beam. He would having nothing below him but the treacherous waters of the channel, more than 200 feet down.

The two men decided to do something about the problem. In June of 1936, before roadway construction began, they ordered a huge trapeze net like circus performers use. This rope net was built onto a steel frame so it extended ahead of the work area and ten feet to either side.

The net was Joseph Strauss's most important contribution to safe bridge building. Never before had bridge builders used a safety net. Since then it has become standard practice.

These ironworkers on a box girder *were securing a set of suspender ropes. The box girders went into place first during roadway construction. They became the sides of the roadway.*

This is a closer view of suspender ropes attached to a box girder. Riveted to the box girder is a wide floor beam.

In late summer of 1936, steelworkers began to hang *suspender ropes* every fifty feet along the cables. The ropes were made of twisted wire and were almost three inches thick. The wire ropes would support the roadway, but until they were fastened to girders they dangled in the wind like socks on a clothesline.

Steel parts for the roadway came by barge from a storage yard thirty miles away on the east shore of San Francisco Bay. Derricks on stationary barges at the base of each tower hoisted the heavy steel up to the roadway level. There, movable derricks on temporary steel tracks set the girders and stiffening trusses and beams where they were needed. Riveting gangs followed to permanently rivet the pieces together. Side girders went into place first, to be fastened every fifty feet to a suspender rope. Every twenty-five feet, a floor beam was placed crosswise between the side girders.

The steel beams called stringers *provided a temporary track for the derrick to run along as it moved ahead to extend the roadway.*

Cables coming down from the south tower passed through the arch above Fort Point, went through the pylons supporting the south end of the bridge, and were then secured to eyebars in the anchorages.

To balance the pull on the cables, roadways had to be built out from both sides of both towers at the same time. The pull on the cables had to be equal all the time. This meant there were four work areas—two working toward the middle of the span, and two working toward the two shores. Sometimes one crew had a problem, and it had to slow down or stop. Immediately it signaled the other three crews to slow down or stop too. Otherwise the uneven pull on the cables would make the towers sway unevenly, throwing off all of the precise calculations.

The riveting crews liked working on the roadway more than in the tower. Here they did their job in the open air.

Rivets did not have to travel through pneumatic tubes. Heaters could toss the hot rivets directly to catchers, who, in turn, gave them to the bucker-ups.

Always the safety nets stayed ahead of the work areas. New sections of net were laced on as needed. With the safety net below them, the crews worked fast. Panel by panel, the roadway grew.

On shore, people shared the excitement. For a long time, they had watched construction of the approach roads leading to the bridge. But now, they could see the roadway on the bridge itself. They watched the derricks on the main span move closer and closer together. They saw the derricks on the side spans move closer to the two shores. Newspapers reported as the gap at mid-span shrank day by day.

Bad weather did not slow the steady pace. A storm one afternoon produced swells as high as fifteen feet. A barge moored at one of the towers was tossed so violently its lines broke. The barge floated out with the tide. It was heading for the open sea before a tugboat finally caught up and towed it back.

By late fall, the concrete approach roads on both shores were finished and the roadway steelwork on the bridge was nearly finished. There had been no serious accidents. Unfortunately, on October 21, a fitting pulled loose on one of the derricks on the main span. A piece of the derrick fell, killing a man. The other workers were sent home for the day. No one knew what caused the accident. But the men agreed—on bridges, those things just happen sometimes.

The next day all the crews were back on their jobs. Work on the roadway continued.

By the middle of November, the side spans had reached the shore. At mid-bridge, the two sections of roadway were separated by a gap of only 100 feet.

With the gap closed between the two sections of the midspan, the retreating derrick and its crews added more steel bracing to the roadway.

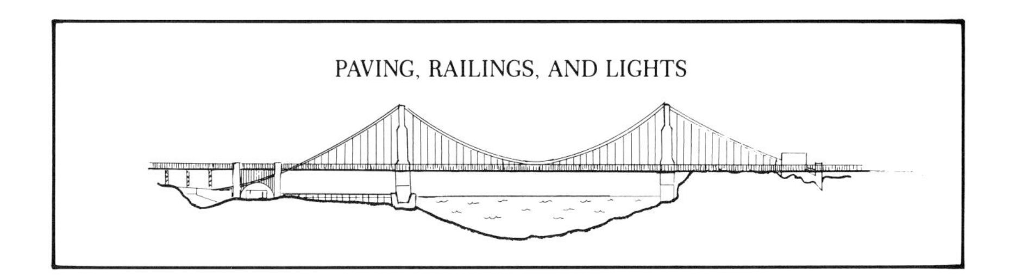

Finishing Touches

On November 18, 1936, a San Francisco newspaper announced in big headlines: "GAP ON GOLDEN GATE SPAN WILL BE CLOSED TODAY."

People hardly needed a paper to tell them the good news. For five months, from both shores, the excited bridge watchers had seen that steel roadway grow longer by the day.

A ceremony was to be held on the main span to celebrate the linking of north and south shores at last. The commandant of Fort Baker and representatives from the Redwood Empire Association walked from the north end of the bridge to a place near the middle and waited. Facing them, on the south side of the gap, were officials from San Francisco. Both groups stood a safe distance back from the gap.

Joseph Strauss took over the controls of the derrick. While the officials watched, he picked up the final 100-foot section of steel. Slowly he lowered the heavy girder. As Strauss eased the section down, the two workmen, called connectors, grabbed it. They fit it in place like the last piece in a puzzle and quickly set drift pins to hold it.

"That's it!" said one of the connectors.

With that, the Golden Gate was officially bridged.

The dignitaries called out greetings to one another. They waved, but none dared step on the newly installed panel to shake hands.

Newspaper sellers shouted the news. People north and south of the Golden Gate cheered. Joseph Strauss had a special reason to feel happy. With the roadway in, the most dangerous parts of the project were behind him. And the bridge had claimed but one life.

The derricks that had raced toward the center of the span now began to retreat as they laid steel forms for curbs and sidewalks and put down more steel *stringers*—the parallel steel beams like the ones the derricks used for tracks. Derricks on the side spans did the same, moving away from the anchorages and toward the towers. Carpenters built wooden forms for pouring concrete, and then flatcars rode over the temporary tracks to bring concrete to pave the roadway.

To keep the weight balanced, concrete was set in sections. Again crews in all four work areas worked at the same pace. They installed *expansion joints* of steel and copper every fifty feet, to allow the steel underneath the paving to expand or contract.

By January 19, 1937, much of the roadway was paved. Cleanup crews, working beneath the roadway from scaffolds, began to remove the wooden forms. Suddenly there

Workers laid plywood over the steel beams before the concrete for the roadway was poured. Marin County is visible in the background.

were loud popping sounds, like gunshots. A heavy scaffold with twelve workers on it had broken loose. It had crashed into the safety net. The popping sounds had been the net snapping loose from its steel frame under the weight of the ten-ton scaffold. Net and workers plunged into the sea. Two men were saved, but ten were lost.

Later, a memorial service was held for the ten and for the worker who had been killed a few months before. A plaque with the men's names was set into a concrete post at the entrance to the bridge. Now the bridge itself was a tribute to their work.

Welders welded reinforcing iron bars over the plywood sections to strengthen the paved roadway.

Architect Irving Morrow designed open railings so motorists could enjoy the view. If a motorist drove at a reasonable speed, the vertical bars of the railings blurred together so that the Pacific Ocean and San Francisco Bay were visible. But if a driver moved too slowly the vertical bars blocked the view. This kept traffic flowing smoothly.

At a hearing it was determined that the scaffold had fallen because safety bolts were undersized. After that, there were no more accidents as finishing touches were added to the bridge.

Lights and railings were installed. They were designed by Irving Morrow, the architect who had designed the towers. Morrow liked to create things that were attractive to look at and pleasant to use. His open railings, unusual in bridge design, allowed motorists crossing the bridge to enjoy the view of the Pacific Ocean to the west and the San Francisco Bay to the east.

The lights were sodium vapor, something very new in street lighting. These special lamps gave off a yellowish glow to provide motorists with better visibility in the fog.

Approaches had to be built so motorists could get onto the bridge. The approach road on the Marin side was difficult and expensive to construct. In the upper right-hand corner of the photograph is Sausalito, the town in Marin County where the ferry from San Francisco docked.

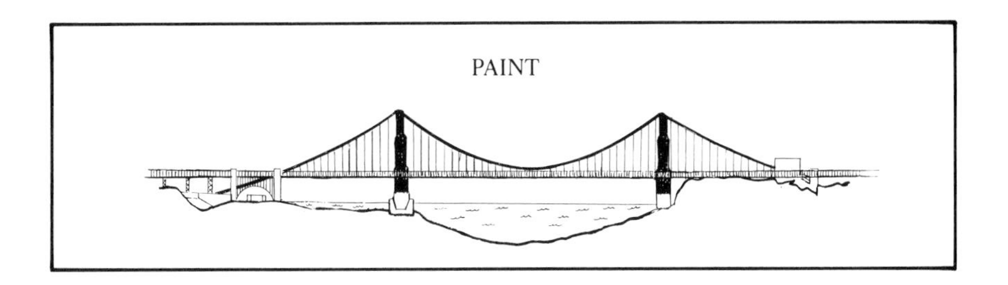

The Golden Rivet

When a young tourist from the East saw the Golden Gate Bridge for the first time, she was surprised and a bit disappointed. "But it isn't gold!" she said.

During construction many San Franciscans had wanted the bridge over the Golden Gate to be painted gold, in honor of its name. Joseph Strauss's staff architect, Irving Morrow, considered gold.

But first he tested paint samples of many colors. He set them on top of Fort Point, facing west. They were exposed to fog, wind, rain, and salt air—the bridge's greatest enemies. Morrow then chose the color that stood up best, international orange, and to this day the bridge across the Golden Gate is painted international orange. This color was easiest to see in dense fog. Morrow felt it would go well with the brown and green hills circling the bay, the blue water and sky, and the reddish cliffs of Marin.

To give the suspender cables their final coat of international orange, painters sat in bosun's chairs, *wooden boards slung from ropes. At the right time of day, the sun's rays can change the reddish-orange color so it truly* does *look golden.*

"Too modern," grumbled some critics. They favored black or gray or silver—colors they were used to seeing on bridges. Local artist and sculptor Benny Bufano disagreed. He wrote to bridge officials praising Morrow's choice.

"The color," Bufano said, "adds to the great beauty and color symphony of the hills."

Painting of the steel parts began in the summer of 1933. If left untreated, steel will corrode almost immediately from the salt air. With buckets and brushes, the painters applied two protective undercoats to every inch of steel—towers, cables, suspender ropes, and roadway steel. Then they gave everything a final coat of international orange. That first paint job used more than 10,000 gallons of paint.

Though the paint is not gold, there is gold in the bridge. On April 28, 1937, two weeks after the roadway was paved, Joseph Strauss led a group of dignitaries to the center span. It was time for a ceremony to mark the end of the steel work. The final rivet would be gold.

A California businessman donated a pound of gold and cast the rivet. The gold came from the mother lode, where forty-niners had swarmed during the gold rush.

After San Francisco's Mayor Rossi and Joseph Strauss made speeches, a riveter nicknamed Iron Horse stepped forward. He had set the first rivet in the bridge. Now he had been selected to set the last one.

Iron Horse applied his rivet gun and his bucker-up backed the gold rivet. Though riveter and bucker-up worked hard, the gold rivet would not form the same way as a hot steel rivet. The men gave up. Long after the crowd had gone, Iron Horse and his partner quietly finished the job.

All that remained was general cleanup. Equipment had to be installed in the toll plaza. Then the bridge would be open for traffic.

On Pedestrian Day the people had the bridge to themselves. Though the wind blew a few hats away, no one seemed to mind.

A Week of Firsts

The Golden Gate Bridge was finished on Wednesday, May 26, 1937. The next day was Pedestrian Day. Between six in the morning and six that night, 200,000 people strolled, ran, danced, hopped, and skipped across their new bridge.

Eager crowds were at the bridgeheads before sunrise. To claim a place at the head of the line on the San Francisco side, a Boy Scout spent the night there in his sleeping bag.

It cost a nickel to walk across the bridge that first day and another nickel to walk back. Pedestrians who wanted a souvenir could buy a fancy round-trip ticket for a quarter. Toll takers couldn't keep up with crowds surging through the turnstiles.

"Forget the coin collection boxes," they shouted, and shoved out buckets instead, to catch people's coins.

Some pedestrians were in no hurry to get across. They ambled from one side to the other. They felt the rivets. They looked at the magnificent view of the Pacific Ocean to the west, San Francisco Bay to the east.

Navy ships and fishing boats sailed beneath the bridge. Crews on deck waved up at the people at the rail who waved back.

Families spread out picnic lunches in the middle of the roadway. Others bought hot dogs from vendors. That day, according to one estimate, 7,660 feet of hot dogs were sold.

It was like an old-fashioned Fourth of July celebration.

By the time the day was over, security officers had rescued hundreds of cameras, hats, and purses that fell or were dropped into the safety net below. The ambulance attendants at each end of the bridge had treated forty walkers with blisters on the Marin side and thirteen walkers with blisters on the San Francisco side.

Everyone wanted to be the first to do something on the new bridge. When security officers started to help a woman who looked as if she were sick, they found she was trying to be the first to cross the bridge with her tongue hanging out.

There were other firsts.

Two sisters on roller skates left their San Francisco house at three in the morning so they could be at the bridge when it opened. They wanted to claim the title of "first to skate across."

It was not clear whether a Scottie, or a dachshund named Fritz, was the first dog to cross the bridge. There were also the first twins to cross, the first stilt-walker, the first mother pushing a baby in a stroller. Kids and grown-ups shared in the fun. There was the first to cross barefoot, the first musician tooting a tuba.

The bridge had its own special voice.

In the afternoon, a man held up his hand. "Be quiet," he told the crowd. "Listen to the bridge."

They did. Here is how a newspaper reported the strange event: "A hush fell on the crowd. They stood still—and heard the voice of the bridge!...Away down, a deep roar ...high up in the wires, a shrill sound...different notes, changing, deepening, rising...."

The bridge was a giant wind harp.

The next day, automobiles had their turn. Early in the morning, city officials climbed in cars and boarded the

Caravans from as far north as Canada and Alaska came to the opening on May 28, 1937. There was a brief traffic jam when it was finally opened to motorists, but eventually everyone got onto the bridge.

ferry from San Francisco to Sausalito. At the approach road on the Marin side the cars lined up, waiting for the official motorcade to begin.

But first, there were ceremonial barriers to get through.

Two enormous redwood logs blocked the approach. While the cars waited, champion log sawers from California, Washington, and Idaho competed to see who could saw through the logs first. A Washington man was the first to saw through one of the logs and open the roadway. He won a $500 prize.

The cars moved on to encounter chains of copper, silver, and gold festooned across the bridge. While camera shutters clicked all around them, officials cut through the chains with welding torches.

At last the motorcade drove across the bridge. At the San Francisco end, Fiesta Queens in long, ruffly dresses stood in a row holding hands. They blocked the roadway until Joseph Strauss officially presented the completed bridge to the Golden Gate Bridge and Highway District.

"This bridge needs [no] praise," said the chief engineer softly. "It speaks for itself. We who have labored long are grateful. What Nature rent asunder long ago, man has joined today...."

With that, the Fiesta Queens stepped aside to let the motorcade proceed.

It was almost noon.

On the dot of twelve, California time, President of the United States Franklin D. Roosevelt pressed a telegraph key in his White House office. It signaled that the Golden Gate Bridge was officially opened to motor traffic.

Motorists waiting at the approaches on both sides of the bridge began honking car horns. All over San Francisco and in Marin County, church bells rang out. People cheered.

Right: *Joseph Strauss, in the dark overcoat, stood next to a top-hatted dignitary and San Francisco's mayor, who was dressed in formal wear with a bowler hat and a white carnation in his lapel. This was one of the many ceremonies on opening day.*

Below: *To cut the silver chain, one of the ceremonial barriers, San Francisco's Mayor Rossi donned goggles and leather gloves and melted it with a welding torch.*

In the harbor, foghorns bellowed. From ocean liners and freighters, tugboats and navy ships, bells clanged and whistles sounded.

Five hundred navy combat planes flew overhead in salute. Beneath the bridge steamed thirty-eight ships of the United States Navy. Police cars and fire trucks from both sides roared over the bridge, sirens shrieking. Close behind, came the stream of motorists.

On that first day, 32,300 cars crossed the Golden Gate Bridge. Drivers had to pay a fifty-cent toll for car, driver,

A huge motorcade, with cars six abreast, moved across the bridge from Marin County to officially open the bridge. After that, automobiles from both directions could cross the bridge.

and four passengers. Each extra passenger had to pay a nickel. People marveled at the wide, modern highway—three lanes in each direction!

The fiesta to celebrate the opening of the Golden Gate Bridge lasted a week. There were pageants and games and parties. Movie actor Robert Taylor came up from Hollywood to crown the Fiesta Queen. Singer Al Jolson serenaded the crowds with "California, Here I Come!" There were concerts, fancy dress balls, and torchlight parades. Amid popping firecrackers the New Year's ceremonial dragon danced its way through the streets of Chinatown. In Marin County, crowds held community sings, danced in the streets, and shot off fireworks.

Because his work was done, Joseph Strauss resigned his job as chief engineer. He had expected the project to take four years and cost $35 million. Despite all the unexpected delays and extra expenses, he finished only five months late and under budget. There was $1,334,000 left over, even after all the bills were paid and bondholders had been given the interest their bonds had earned during the construction years.

Besides his fee of a little over $1 million, Mr. Strauss received from the Bridge District a gold pass to cross the bridge free as often as he wished.

Joseph Strauss had little chance to use his lifetime gold pass. Less than a year later, the man who built the Golden Gate Bridge died.

And Since Then...

From the start, the people of San Francisco considered this new bridge to be "their" bridge. They loved it so much that in 1939 they held an exposition to honor both the Golden Gate Bridge and its sister span, the newly built Bay Bridge that connects San Francisco and Oakland, to the east.

Soon, the Golden Gate Bridge became San Francisco's unofficial trademark. Two years later, the United States entered the Second World War. The bridge became a national symbol, as well.

During the war, navy ships steamed out to sea under the bridge. They carried supplies and troops headed for action in the Pacific. Battleships, destroyers, and aircraft carriers jammed San Francisco Harbor. At night, bridge lights were turned off and motorists had to dim their headlights, so they wouldn't provide a beacon for any lurking submarines or enemy planes.

Later, as troops came back from action in the Pacific, the familiar twin towers of the Golden Gate Bridge symbolized "home, at last!" To waiting families perched on the bluffs overlooking the Gate, no sight was more welcome than those troopships returning under the Golden Gate Bridge.

The Golden Gate Bridge has seen changes over the decades. In the fifties, officials began to worry after a suspension bridge in Washington State twisted in a high wind and broke. They consulted Clifford Paine. He recommended cross-bracing under the roadway of the Golden Gate Bridge. Though the bridge was still sound, this was done as a precaution.

By the seventies, there were more changes. Pedestrian turnstiles were removed. People no longer paid to walk on the bridge and bicyclists could now ride their bikes across, instead of walking them. On weekends bicyclists must use the west sidewalk. On weekdays they share the east sidewalk with pedestrians, who always have to stay on that side.

In 1971 the bridge had earned enough in tolls to pay off its loan. It had been thirty-eight years. Since then, the money collected in tolls has paid for maintenance.

The Golden Gate Bridge maintains a sizeable service force. Some you can see every day, such as the toll-takers. Often tow trucks haul sick cars off the bridge or deliver gasoline to motorists who run out of gas in mid-span. Many service personnel you may not see. There are security officers and fire fighters. There is also a large staff of inspectors who scramble up the towers and along the cables looking for signs of corrosion. The maintenance force includes ironworkers, electricians, and of course, painters!

Other bridges can now claim to be the world's longest or tallest—titles the Golden Gate Bridge held for seventeen years. But few bridges are as well loved by people the world over. Those living close to the bridge are especially loyal. This was proved in 1972, when, despite the painters' best efforts, salt air had corroded the suspension cables. The company hired to replace the cables hung its sign on the bridge. The people of San Francisco were angry. They objected to an ugly sign marring the beauty of their bridge. They threatened to sue unless the sign came down. It did—right away!

Weather has forced the bridge to close only three times. And this was to protect motorists from high winds, which can cause a car to swerve across three lanes. Over the radio, *wind warnings* are occasionally issued. People in campers and lightweight cars are advised to stay off the bridge because the strong winds might blow them out of their lane.

As the bridge neared its fiftieth birthday, the roadway needed repair. The resurfacing project cost more than the original cost of the entire bridge. By this time there was so much traffic on the bridge that the crews replacing the roadway and sidewalk had to work at night, so they would not disrupt traffic too much. They finished in plenty of time for the Golden Gate Bridge's glorious fiftieth anniversary celebration.

Every year, the number of cars using the Golden Gate Bridge grows larger. The billionth car crossed the bridge in 1985. By then, the ferries had started running again. Now many commuters from the north choose to ride the ferry across the Golden Gate. The reason: They want to avoid rush hour traffic on the bridge!

Near the spot where Joseph Strauss dreamed of building the "impossible" bridge nearly three-quarters of a century ago, there now stands a bronze statue of the "small man with big ideas."

Joseph Strauss would be surprised, since a half century ago it was his bridge that put the ferries out of business. Something else might amaze Mr. Strauss, were he alive today. Tourists by the thousands, from all parts of the world, come every day of the year to admire his masterpiece.

On the other hand, maybe Mr. Strauss would take it in stride. During those years when he fought to build his bridge a critic asked how long he expected his bridge to last.

Joseph Strauss had replied calmly, "Forever!"

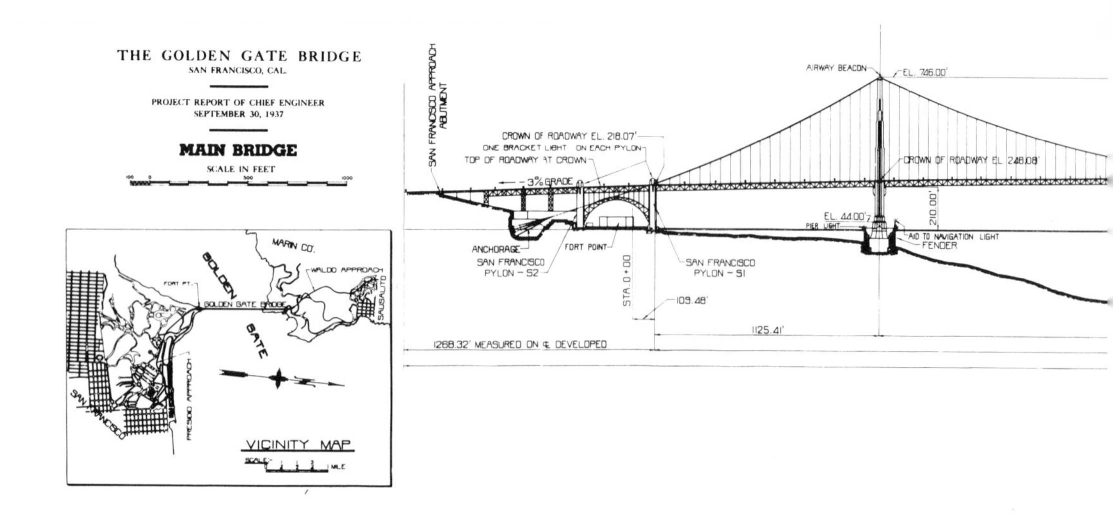

Facts and Figures

Length of main span	4,200 ft.	1,280 m
Length of each side span	1,125 ft.	343 m
Length of entire suspended structure	6,450 ft.	1,966 m
Width of bridge	90 ft.	27.4 m
Maximum sideways bend, center	27.7 ft.	8.4 m
Maximum downward bend, center span	10.8 ft.	3.3 m
Maximum upward bend, center span	5.8 ft.	1.8 m
Clearance above water	220 ft.	67 m
Height of towers above water	746 ft.	227 m
Weight of two towers	88,800,000 lbs.	40,300,000 kg
Load on tower from cable	123,000,000 lbs.	56,000,000 kg
Diameter of wire	0.196 in.	5 mm
Total length of wire used	80,000 miles	129,000 km
Concrete in south pier and fender	130,000 cu.yds.	99,400 m
Concrete in north pier	23,500 cu.yds.	18,000 m
Concrete in anchorages and pylons	182,000 cu.yds.	139,100 m
Concrete in approaches and paving	53,500 cu.yds.	40,900 m
Steel in each tower	44,400 tons	40,280,000 kg
Steel in suspended structure	24,000 tons	21,770,000 kg
Steel in anchorages	4,400 tons	3,990,000 kg

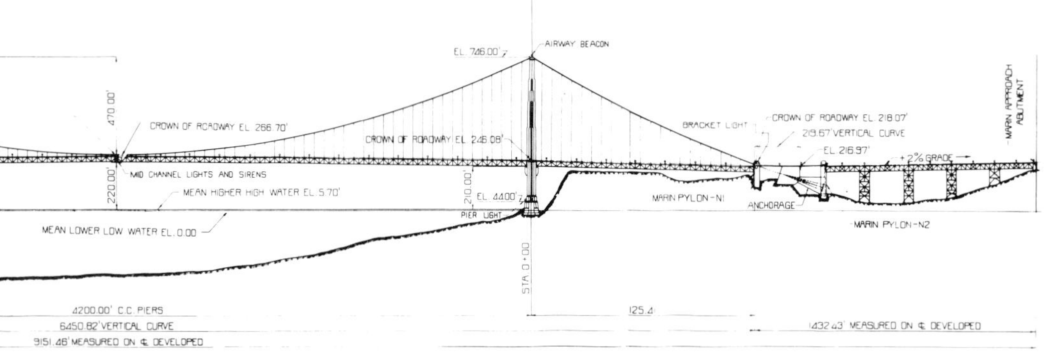

Bibliography

Billings, Henry B. *Bridges.* New York: Viking, 1956

Brown, Allen. *Golden Gate.* Garden City, New York: Doubleday & Co., 1965

Cassady, Stephen. *Spanning the Gate.* Mill Valley, California: Squarebooks, 1979

Chester, Michael. *Joseph Strauss, Builder of the Golden Gate Bridge.* New York: G. P. Putnam's Sons, 1965

Dillon, Richard. *High Steel.* Millbrae, California: Celestial Arts, 1979

Fritz, Jean. *San Francisco.* New York: Rand McNally, 1962

Gilliam, Harold. *San Francisco Bay.* Garden City, New York: Doubleday & Co., 1957

Goldwater, Daniel. *Bridges and How They Are Built.* New York: Young Scott, 1965

Jackson, Charlotte. *The Story of San Francisco.* New York: Random House, 1955

Jackson, David. *The Wonderful World of Engineering.* Garden City, New York: Doubleday & Co., 1969

Jacobs, David and Neville, Anthony. *Bridges, Canals and Tunnels.* New York: American Heritage Co., Inc., Smithsonian Library, 1968

Phillips, Catherine Coffin. *Through the Golden Gate.* San Francisco: Sutton House, 1938

Strauss, Joseph. *Report of the Chief Engineer to Board of Directors of Golden Gate Bridge and Highway District.* San Francisco, 1937.

Wolman, Baron and Horton, Tom. *Superspan.* Mill Valley, California: Squarebooks, 1984

Index

Credits

Drawings: Meg Pelta, pp. 8, 16, 23, 27, 33, 43, 53, 61, 69, 75, 79; Golden Gate Bridge, Highway & Transportation District, pp. 92-93
Photographs: Archives of Golden Gate Bridge, Highway & Transportation District, Charles Hiller, photographer, pp. 2-3, 29, 32, 42, 52, 55, 56, 58, 59, 60, 72, 76, 78, 83 (bottom), 84; San Francisco Archives, pp. 6, 54; San Francisco Maritime Museum, pp. 10, 11; Redwood Empire Association, pp. 13, 14, 30, 31, 34, 46, 49, 50 (both photos), 63, 64, 65, 66, 68, 71, 73, 74, 81, 83 (top); California Historical Society, San Francisco, p. 19; Peter Stackpole, p. 22; California Historical Society, San Francisco, Ted Huggins, photographer, pp. 36, 39; Edmond Pelta, pp. 86, 90
Other (facsimile of bond): Archives of Golden Gate Bridge, Highway & Transportation District, p. 25

Front cover photograph by Orville Andrews
Back cover photographs by Peter Stackpole and (inset) by California Historical Society, San Francisco